DARTMOUTH

A VISUAL REMEMBRANCE

Jack...
your volunteer service
is tremendously appreciated.
Thank you for all you did
to help assure the success
of the campaign for Dartmouth.

Photography by George Robinson
Introduction by David Bradley

Copyright © 1982 by Russell A. Boss
All rights reserved
Edited by James B. Patrick
Designed by Donald G. Paulhus
ISBN 0-940078-06-6
Printed in Japan
Published by Foremost Publishers, Inc.
Little Compton, R.I. 02837

The assistance of
Russell A. Boss, '61
and members of the
Dartmouth College community
in the publication of this book
is greatly appreciated.

Leaf Kicking

Of course there is music. There was always music and words and singing, memories and visions like a wind-harvest on a bright October day.

That's what these pictures are all about, a new harvest by the photographer George Robinson. Robinson's an adopted Vermonter; we can trust him with the images. In this book he is inviting us to go out on a leaf-kicking expedition with him.

I propose to accept, see what I can turn up.

*

First thing I notice in these pictures are the happy, young faces of the modern Dartmouth. Everything good under the sun is here: the libraries, the laboratories, the teachers, the leisure time for exploring and learning in the long white afternoons or solitary midnights.

This is a prosperous Dartmouth, now in its 3rd century. Still a small college, with a multitude of those who love it.

Nothing of the log-cabin school carved from a wilderness two hundred years ago remains. Nothing of the raw provincial college of a hundred years ago remains, when cows and horses had to be chased from the green so that baseball could be played.

Nothing but the shape of the hills, the north-south sliding gleam of the river, and the spirit of the place.

The spirit hasn't changed much in two centuries. The prototype Dartmouth student wrote his shout from the hills in the third year of the College. His words could have served as the Freshman Handbook in 1772; they would do pretty well today:

I took my axe with me, and such articles of clothing and a few such books as were necessary . . .

Something happens to young men and women up here. It can't be preached or planned for or taught; it just happens:

Maybe on a Freshman trip where, scrambling over the slabs of a shattered ridge on Washington or Passaconaway, they suddenly find themselves looking across 10,000 years into the face of the ice age;

Or, crowding into a classroom for the first time, they hear all the impossible things expected of them: the books to learn, the experiments, computers, research, the papers — the thinking they'll have to do. (Milton, for example. Has anyone yet figured out what to think about Milton?);

Or discovering the books of Baker Library, the arts of Hopkins Center;

Or alone some midnight, standing in the great white cold among five billion years of stars —

Something happens. When we next hear of these people, they've been exploring the Ross ice shelf or on the beaches of the Sandwich Islands, paddling the Dubawnt or forcing a route on the west ridge of Everest, inventing a kidney machine or writing a book of poems.

*

But of all unexpected things, the oddest is this: that there was ever a Dartmouth College in this place.

Take a tiny Indian school in Connecticut, declare it to be a college, uproot it, lug it (along with a handful of Delawares and Mohawks) two hundred miles north in carts and wagons, beyond all reach of civilization, beyond the Deerfield settlements and Fort No. 4, to a wilderness riverbank in the Hampshire Grants —

Tuck Mall and Baker Library.

12 – Crabapple blossoms and bicycle rack.

13 – Birch bark and paperbacks.

14 – Class Day custom: seniors shatter clay pipes on ancient Pine stump.

15 – Testing the filtering action of an earlier era.

16 – Crewing the Connecticut River.

17 – Dartmouth Hall — and springtime.

Heathery hillside.

20 – Baker Library perspective.

21 – Meditative moment in Sanborn Library.

22 – Card catalogs in window embrasures.

23 – Researcher with ball point pen.

24 – Spiralling iron balustrade marks west entrance of
	Baker Library.

25 – Mosaic of blooms borders patio at Hanover Inn.

Hot air balloon — a pre-flight peek at Dartmouth Hall.

28 – Ivied escape.
29 – Baker Library — main corridor.

30 – From the song of the same name.

31 – Slaloming with a kayak.

32 – Tower clock — Baker Library.
33 – The steps at Murdough Center.

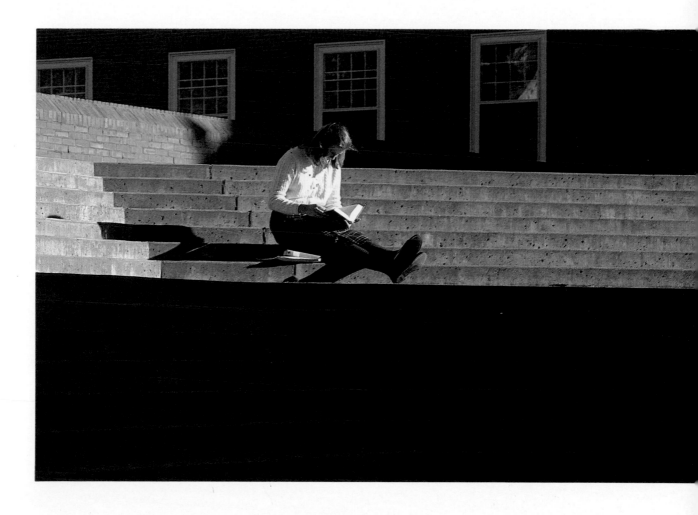

34 – Reward for the climb.

35 – Tranquil drifting on the Connecticut River.

36 – Circular shadows on patterned brickwalk.

37 – Baker Library dormers line up beneath clock tower.

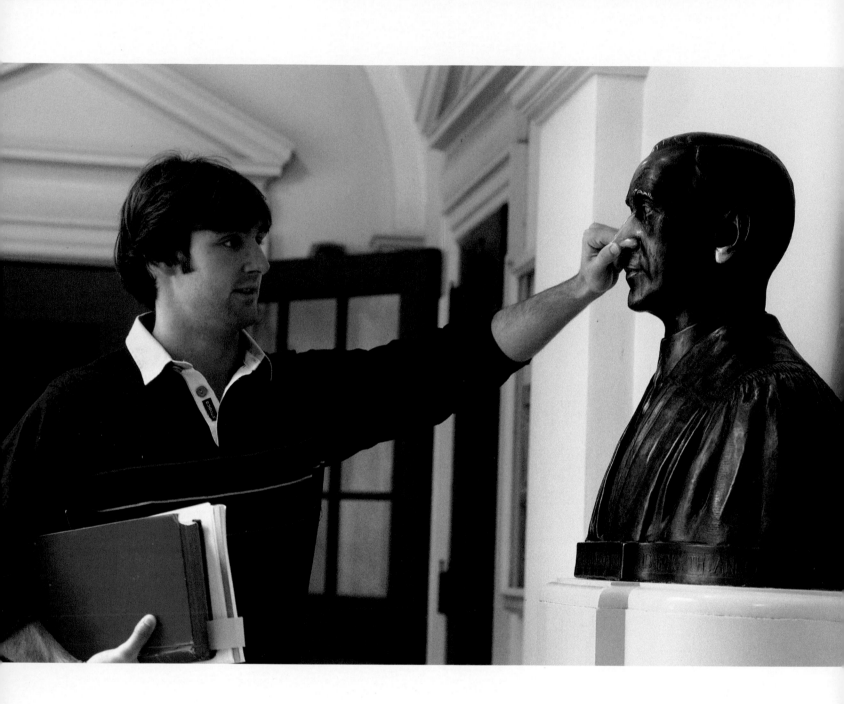

38 – Rubbing the nose for luck.

39 – Bust (and nose) of Dean Craven Laycock.

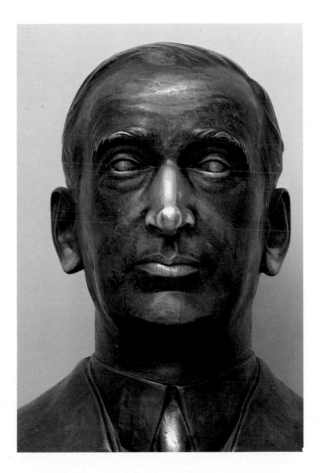

40 – Southward from Fairchild Science Center to Baker
Library Tower.

41 – Carpenter Art Gallery.

42 – On the lawn before Baker Library.

43 – Rainbow over Reed Hall.

44 – Postered entryway at Thayer Hall.

45 – Keyboard antics at Hopkins Center.

46 – Mid-Term weekend.

47 – Temporary tangle in a trout stream.

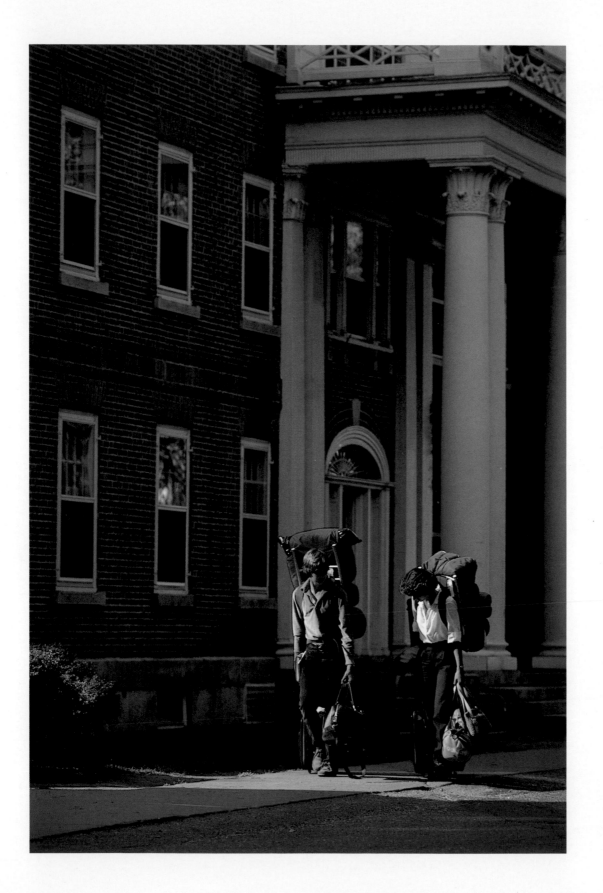

In Baker Library: Cyrus Dallin's unforgettable "Appeal to the Great Spirit."

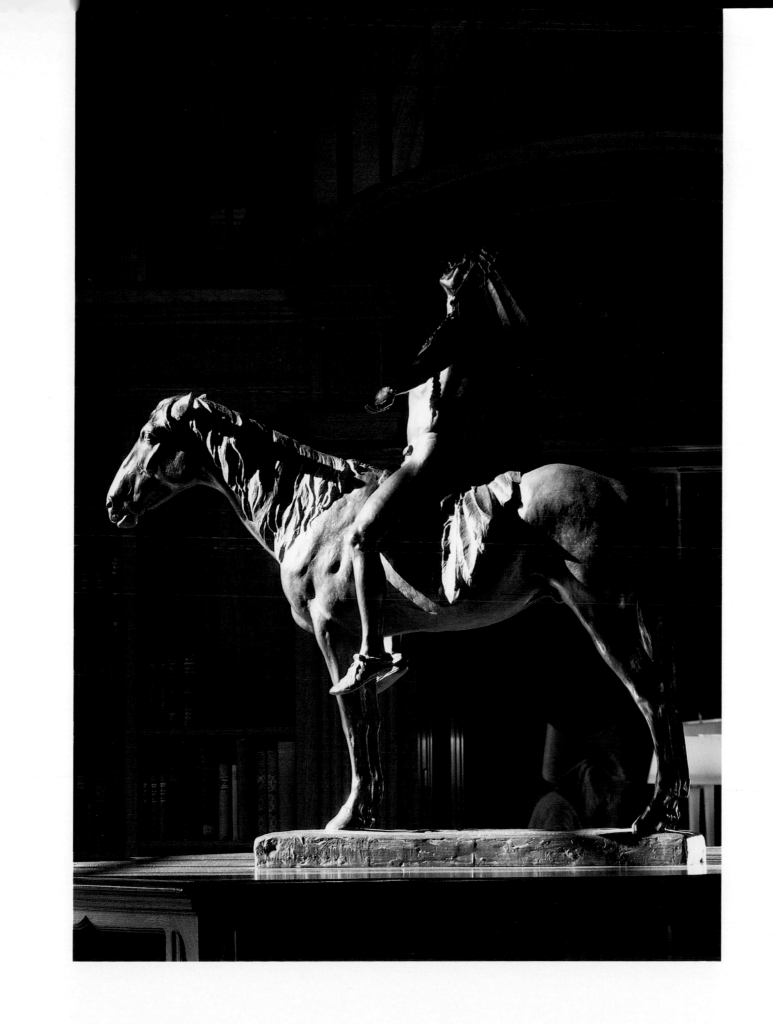

50 – Windsurfer with bright yellow sail.

51 – Coffee and Shakespeare in an arched alcove. Sanborn
   English Library.

52 – Classic facade of Dartmouth Hall reflects the gold of
autumn sun.

53 – Stately clock with gilded dial, Baker Library.

54 – Metallic makeup for "Wizard of Oz" in Hopkins Center.

55 – Afternoon rehearsal in Webster Hall.

Nestling towers, autumnal hills.

58 – Campus bonfire.

59 – Student seating.

60 – And focusing, like shafted sunlight, on the page.

61 – Gracefully arched mullions of Baker Library windows.

62 – Slumbrous anticipation.

63 – And the fresh air appetite.

64 – Leafy texture lends an almost oriental air to Sherman
  Fairchild Physical Sciences Center.

65 – Ornithological delights in paneled Tower Room,
  Baker Library.

66 – Field Hockey huddles — Chase Field.

67 – White on white, at the bubbler.

67

68 – Professor James Epperson Memorial Benches.

69 – Autumnal mist.

70 – Controlling form, Hopkins Center.

71 – Fall carpeting on Dartmouth Row.

74 – Momentary stillness in Wentworth Hall.

75 – Scarlet ivy forms brilliant pattern on aged brick.

76 – Leaf-flecked pools, perfectly still beside tumbling stream.

77 – Rock climbers.

"THIS, SIR, IS MY CASE! IT IS THE CASE NOT MERE-
LY OF THAT HUMBLE INSTITUTION, IT IS THE CASE
OF EVERY COLLEGE IN OUR LAND!...IT IS, SIR, AS
I HAVE SAID, A SMALL COLLEGE. AND YET..."

78 – Student's left hand unconsciously mimics that of
Daniel Webster in Thayer Hall painting.

79 – Hand carved seal of Dartmouth.

82 – Mountain vista.

83 – Expectant rockers — the porch at Hanover Inn.

84 – Gallery encounter at Memorial Field.

85 – Seasonal texture.

The brilliant birch trees of Occum Pond.

88 – Gallery conversation.
89 – Alone in Baker Library.

90 – Baronial dining room at Tuck School.

91 – Scrutiny of wooden figure at Hopkins Center.

Solitary skier.

94 – Snow-swaddled repose, Dartmouth Cemetery.

95 – Dartmouth Hall: study in whites and grays with vertical blacks.

96 – Energizing eclecticism of a professor's office.

97 – Dartmouth Hall through winter tracery.

98 – Knit cap collection nears top on Dartmouth Skiway.

99 – Chopping ice beneath dazzling dome of Dartmouth Hall.

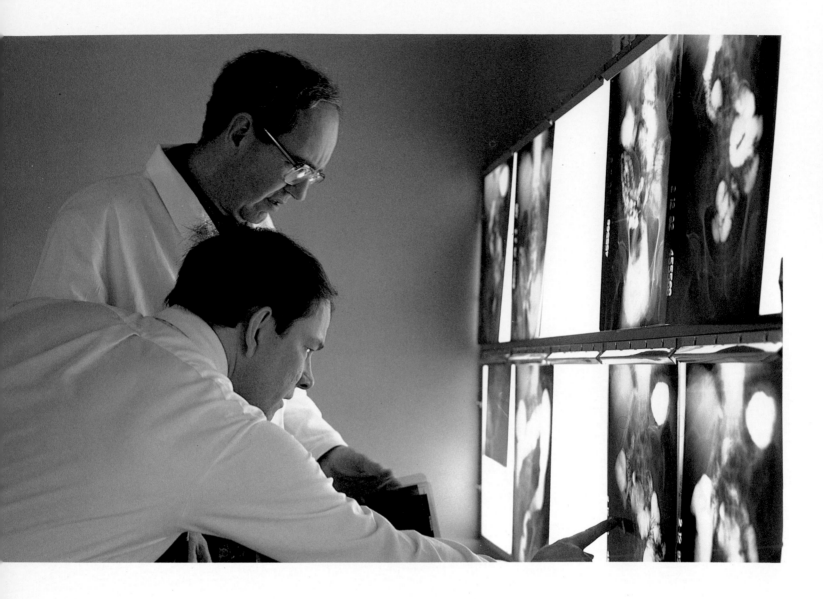

100 – In a sober light at Dartmouth Medical School.

101 – Fitting symbol for the college infirmary.

102 – Tuck Mall, freshly plowed, leads way to classicly proportioned Baker Library.

103 – Roof relief.

104 – Turreted symmetry, Wilson Museum.

105 – Tabletop perspective of Russell R. Larmon '19 Room,
Baker Library

106 – Occum Pond hosts hardy skaters.

107 – The early night of winter, Baker Tower.

108 – Bright red bike basket, Wentworth Hall.

109 – Profiled pony tail in Sanborn Library.

110 – Weather vanes in mute agreement: Baker Tower and
     Church of Christ steeple.

111 – Voices 'neath the rafters of Rollins Chapel.

112 – Antique artistry in Carpenter Hall Gallery.

113 – Icicled gargoyle, Rollins Chapel.

Mount Washington and Tuckerman's Ravine.

116 – Winter carnival offer from Amos Tuck School of
Business Administration.

117 – Maritime motif wins sculpture competition for
Hitchcock Hall.

117

118 – Purpled majesty: Mount Moosilauke.

119 – Shadowed ski trail over the golf course.

120 – Campus Christmas tree.

121 – Rich interior of Thayer Hall frames bleak winterscape.

121

122 – Artistry on a large scale.

123 – Great literature in powdered form.

124 – Giant Slalom — Dartmouth Skiway.

125 – Rollins Chapel provides curvilinear frame for
    Dartmouth Row.

126 – Carolling from cantilevered verandah at Hopkins Center.

127 – Snow-laden wreath outside Sidney Hayward Room of
Hanover Inn.

128 – Contrasting styles at Morton Farm Riding Center.

129 – Reacquaintance in amber-lit barn, Morton Riding Center.

Lamplight on pink blossoms.

132 – Greening of Hanover Golf Course.

133 – Forest ferns border hiking trail.

134 – Orozco Mural at Baker Library has numbing effect on some students.

135 – Top of the Hop — Hopkins Center.

136 – Weathered headstones welcome silent scholar.

137 – Leafy kaleidoscope.

138 – Doorway dialogue at Sanborn Library.

139 – Towering Roman arches of bridge to Tuck School
dwarf cyclist.

140 – Class of '50, in profile.

141 – Senior footwear, Baker Library lawn.